Christmas Memorie

Professional hints & tips for colouring

1 Before you start

To colour up a drawing properly you need to be well prepared. Sit upright with a straight back and posture. Work in natural light or beneath a good light source, but not in direct sunlight. Choose a flat or slightly angled surface to work on. Remove a page from your book and secure it to your surface with tape to prevent it from slipping. You can use the traditional coloured pencils provided, or any water-based paints, or colouring pencils that can be mixed with water to create watercolour effects. Keep a cloth and eraser handy in case you need to make any changes. You are now ready to start.

2 Applying colour

There are many ways to colour a picture – over time you will develop your own method. Taking the front cover image as an example, a good place to start is with the background details such as the sky. 'Cold' colours such as blues and greys will drop back within your picture, whereas 'warm' colours such as reds and yellows will jump forward. Also light shades of any colour tend to drop back and darker shades come forward. Use broader areas of colour for the background first and add the details of colour and shadow later. The main subject of the image should be darker and stronger than the background. The red poinsettia should be painted to show the texture of the leaves, using lighter and darker shades of red. Other features in the foreground, such as the birds, should be highlighted with strong colours, also.

3 Finishing off

Once you have coloured up your picture, stand back and look to see if there are parts that need a bit more work and that it all comes together. It is sometimes better to 'under work' than 'over work' a picture as it may end up being 'muddy' and confused. Take care not to smudge your work and keep finished pictures stored safely in a flat folder. If you are pleased with the result, why not get it framed so that it can be admired by family and friends?